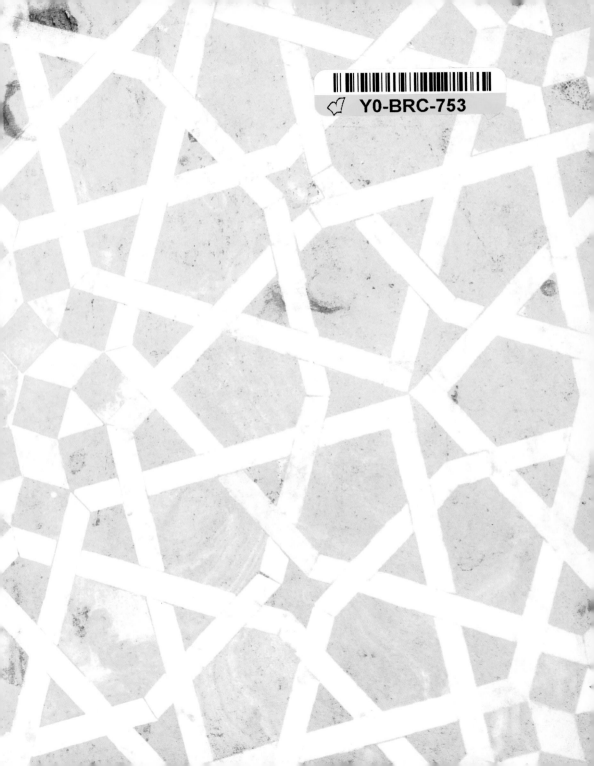

CANVAS OF THE SOUL
MYSTIC POEMS FROM THE HEARTLAND OF ARABIA

15 14 13 12   1 2 3 4

Published by Tughra Books
345 Clifton Ave.
Clifton, New Jersey, 07011, USA

www.tughrabooks.com

Art Director Engin Çiftçi
Graphic Designer Nihat Ince

ISBN: 978-1-59784-269-3

Printed by
Görsel Dizayn Ofset, Istanbul - Turkey

CANVAS
OF THE SOUL

MYSTIC POEMS FROM
THE HEARTLAND OF ARABIA

NIMAH ISMAIL NAWWAB

Go seek a love like this, if you truly live,
Or else remain the slave of time,
And whatever state you seek,
Your lips so dry, must always drink,
Drink up and up,
Till dry lipped still, you reach the source.

For all your skills here given wealth,
Your quest, your handicrafts and works,
Don't they begin in thought,
Begin beside the river?

Jalaluddin al Balkhi Rumi

TABLE OF CONTENTS

FOREWORD by Shems Friedlander

Breath is the essence of life. Drawing is the essence of painting. Typography is the essence of design. Poetry is the essence of literature.

Allah Hu Akbar   (Allah is the Greatest)

Allah Hu Akbar

The call to prayer reverberates over the desert sands and city streets of Saudi Arabia. In the desert the feeling of solitude and quiet, the blanket of stars in an ultramarine sky embraces prayer, while in the city the hustle and clanging of bells and horns, hawkers voices calling for business, requires another kind of dedication. Within the struggle of the traditional to merge with the modern stands the current dilemma of balancing life. Jalaluddin Rumi, the thirteenth century Sufi poet and mystic said: "What kind of prayer is this, when my heart is in the mosque and my mind is in the bazaar."

Ash-hadu an la ilaha illa'Llah

(I bear witness that there is nothing worthy of worship but Allah.)

Ash-hadu an la ilaha illa'Llah

Amidst the traditional and the modern, the desert and the city, the thobe and Gucci, emerges the poetic voice of Nimah Nawwab, born into the lineage of a family of scholars in Makkah. Her poems remind us of the traditional, remind us to remember, remind us to invoke His Name, be it in solitude or in the marketplace.

Ash-hadu anna Muhammadan Rasool Allah

(I bear witness that Muhammad is the Messenger of Allah.)

Ash-hadu anna Muhammadan Rasool Allah

Nawwab has understood, and deftly relates through her poems, the love secreted beneath the skin of one's own dreams and unkept promises. Promises written on the pages of the Book of Man. A constantly changing book that reveals its meaning according to the understanding of the reader. Her poems unfold the living landscapes, the horizons that hold the signs spoken of in the [Koran] Qur'an. The calligraphy of the mountains dipping into the desert, the inkwell of God's words, reflecting the signs before us into the secrets within the Book of Man. This book that has no beginning and no end; this book that is on loan to each and everyone, be they man, woman, or child.

Hayya 'ala as-Salat, Hayya 'ala as-Salat   (Hasten to Prayer)

Hayya 'ala as-Falah, Hayya 'ala as-Falah   (Hasten to Success)

Nawwab's poems speak of the light, the light upon the light, the light within the light, the LIGHT, noorun 'ala noor, the light on the palm of the Prophet Moses revealing the Name of God. Her poems speak of the need to invoke His Name, to realize that every action begins with the hand, upon which is written His Names, so that we may complete the Book of Man, our purpose for being here.

A Sufi sheikh likened prayer and its movements to the reading of the Book of Man. Read. One bows in humility. You are faced with your sins, and your head touches the ground. Allah's greatness is acknowledged and you rise again. And again you are faced with the box of your actions and you bow and place your head to the ground. His Name is breathed and you stand upright.

Nawwab's first published book of poems, "The Unfurling" includes pieces which have been translated into several languages and she became a voice for Arab youth and women. Hers was the first book by a Saudi poet to be published in the U.S. Her interests reach farther than her words. They entwine theatre, music, photography and film. She is determined to invest Saudi youth with an understanding of their own culture, as well as being a bridge to western culture.

"Canvas of the Soul: The Mystic Poems from the Heartland of Arabia," addresses the balance of the inner freedom of one's soul and poses questions of stability between a serene state and walking the tightrope of today's rapidly changing society. Within these pages, scribbled with the inner thoughts of a concerned Arab woman, are seeds of a future being planted now.

Allah Hu Akbar, Allah Hu Akbar   (Allah is the Greatest)

La ilaha illa'Llah (There is nothing worthy of worship but Allah)

La ilaha illa'Llah

Shems Friedlander, Cairo 2011

Shems Friedlander teaches visual communications, drawing, painting and photography at the American University in Cairo. He is the author of nine books and his work has been exhibited worldwide.

10

PREFACE by Dr. Samia Touati

Canvas of the Soul, a unique and stunning collection of profound mystical poems, engage the reader in the dazzling journey of the soul. *Canvas of the Soul* is an allegorical journey of the soul's revelation, longing and quest for a reunion with, to use Nimah Nawwab's terms, the "Beloved" in "What Stops the Joining?"

It is not an easy endeavor to write poetry that evokes the uttermost state of spirituality and transcendence. However, the poet Nimah Nawwab, descending from a scholarly family in Makkah, Saudi Arabia, allows herself the license of scribing the worlds of the seen and the unseen, of the concrete and abstract, of the tangible and the perceived, and of the surface and the deep.

Through her mystic poetry rich with poignant picturesque utterances, Nawwab offers a poetic description which exhilarates the reader's view and imagination. In an attempt to give an account of her elevating experience of the soul, she portrays the high worlds and the panoramic scenes of "gardens," "rivers," "oceans," and "creatures" that chant serenely and silently to celebrate the unique "presence" and "oneness" as in "The Two World Celebrate:"

"The majesty of your Blessings

Birds of prey, birds of peace,

roses, jasmines, lotuses,

grains of sand, rock, boulders

rivers and oceans

silently, stridently mark your presence

Tasabeeh galore..."

Canvas of the Soul reflects to a certain extent the influence of some of the best known mystic poets such as Jalaluddin Rumi, Hafiz and 'Attar on Nimah Nawwab's work. Along with these poets, Nawwab has developed the so-called Sufi poetry which hails its thoughts and ideas from the Qu'ran and Islamic belief and tradition. However, the uniqueness of *Canvas of the Soul* lies in the way Nimah Nawwab has crafted meticulously vivid and worldly imagery to depict the soul's mystical journey; and most importantly, in the way she portrays, par excellence, the various states of her consciousness.

Ya Allah, Subhana Allah

Nimah's poems, at times, invite and engage the soul to join in the journey while at others, they inquire about and probe into the act of seeking the ultimate reunion. The tone of her voice echoes and speaks of the inner world and outer world, prompting the soul trapped in the ever-changing world to slow the pace and engagement to the physical life and perceive the existence of the creator and immaterial life. The voice and tone of voice that shake the inner and urge it for awareness and awakening.

Canvas of the Soul gracefully and gradually reveals the paths of the journey as Nawwab has utilized an endless and inspiring collection of moving words and expressions such as "light/Noor," "inner fire," "internal music of the soul," "schools of Oneness," "chant," "sand," "His Signs," "peace," "concrete manifestations," "beyond," "His Will," "raindrops of blessing," "unified souls," "horizon of Ultimate Unity," ... which intensifies the seeker's embracing of the unique journey. The collection of poems itself flows smoothly in an interwoven way, as the mystic poet Nawwab uses a variety of techniques such as alliteration and foreshadowing to highlight the soul's journey. From the very beginning of her book, she declares "The Celebration of Oneness," then proceeds to engage the soul into a deep descent, then she moves on to raising questions and contemplating prior to sinking into the state of waiting and seeking of "The Ultimate Reunion—The Ultimate Unity" at the eternal world.

Dr. Samia Touati has taught English at Virginia Commonwealth University in Qatar for the past four years; and continues to work actively on research, translation and editing. Samia holds a BA and MA in English Language and Literature majoring in Socio-/Linguistics and Cultural Studies. She has received her Ph.D. in the English Language and Literature-Language and Culture in Contact in 2004 from King Mohammed V University, Rabat, Morocco.

CHAPTER ONE

CELEBRATION OF ONENESS

The Two Worlds Celebrate

The majesty of Your Blessings
birds of prey, birds of peace,
roses, jasmine, lotuses
grains of sand, rock, boulders
rivers and oceans
silently, stridently mark your presence
Tasabih galore
their quiet prayers in Your Honor
rise through the very air we breathe
with every breath we take we breathe You in

Yet the two worlds are divided
in a temporary holding period
till the Final Joining
takes hold in full magnitude

With every heartbeat, soulbeat
we celebrate Your Power and Love
Unity and Love, Love and Mercy embrace us
and we drink from the wine of your creations
                          in blissful, blessed peace.

*Tasabih: invocations

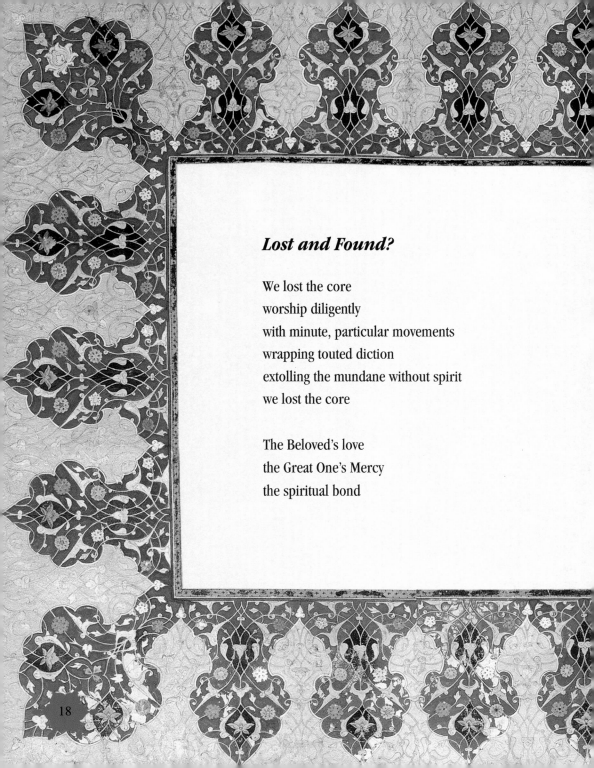

Lost and Found?

We lost the core
worship diligently
with minute, particular movements
wrapping touted diction
extolling the mundane without spirit
we lost the core

The Beloved's love
the Great One's Mercy
the spiritual bond

are out of the equation
we lost the core

Who savors the fruit
and leaves the heart, core,

Reviving the essence
we embrace peace
and are devotees of Higher Love.

The Revered Word

We reside in the land of words and letters
where letters burst forth with every drop of water
poured forth with floods of rain
where letters were birthed with the birthing of humanity
as every word became an island to live on
every word became a wave racing along the coasts
a haven in the scorching heat
a balm under shielding palm trees

As uncharted history unfolded its pages
in reams of forgotten ages
and the world of words rose, amassed, coalesced
through poems and celebrated songs

perfuming the very air
with revered resonance

As the blade of the mighty, magnificent pen
sliced through to conquered reason
carrying forth the message, *the Amanah*,
the Trusted Messenger bore forth
the ultimate of ultimates
in words beyond the ken,
unsurpassed eloquence,
mighty wisdom
in savored, solid passages for mankind
                              to live by and be lived.

*Amanah: trust

Celebration of Oneness

The music soars
chants gloriously celebrate
the wonders of Your Mercy
the Beloved's person revered
'Come, let us celebrate'
let's celebrate
celebrate
the Beauty of the created
embrace the night, the day
of Oneness.

Let's Not Forget

The cup overflows
with the *barakat* of His Grace
let's not forget the next phase

The passions of His worshipers fill up the world
strife, hunger, poverty
abound

Yet His Signs supersede all
with His Mercy and Light
let's not forget the next phase

Without hope, dreams, yearnings
how can we strive for the
    Final and Sought After Meeting?

*Barakat: blessings

Canvas of the Soul

Rising up from the scorched ground
rise up, rise up
bathe yourself
in the raindrops of blessings
step onto the rainbow of serenity
and inhale the aroma of blossoming acceptance
as the canvas of your soul
explodes in radiant colors
beyond our unseeing eyes.

The Plain of Radiance

The nightingale of knowledge ascends
joined in flight across the first river, first ocean
by flocks of doves of grace
alighting on the reborn trees
of lush certainty
along the path of freedom

Path of freedom from ego, from greed
from gossip, from hatred
from named and unnamed evils

As the self perks up
expounds, expands
in fascinated thankfulness
brimming thankfulness
for the revealed radiant Plain of Glory.

Concert of Grace

In the utter silence of the world
of nature unbound
we seek serenity
seek peace
can we ever hear
even a whisper of the praise
given so fully
rising from every mound, tree
bird song, bear roar

A concert of grace performed naturally
by countless known and unknown creatures
as they praise, praise, praise
Your Glory
    subhanak, subhanak, subhanak.

*Subhanak: invocations of The One with this phrase subhanak, connotating a multitude of
gratefulness, wonder and thankfulness

Fire of Creation

The cure was present from the second of inception
of the human and non human birth
the starting points of the felt and unfelt spirits
with creation's inception

Can we ever realize the magnitude
of the single thought, word, action
which stroked the fire of it all?

Can we find each soul's elemental light
sparkling and hidden
blatant and unobtrusive
will the soul's rooting soil be revered?

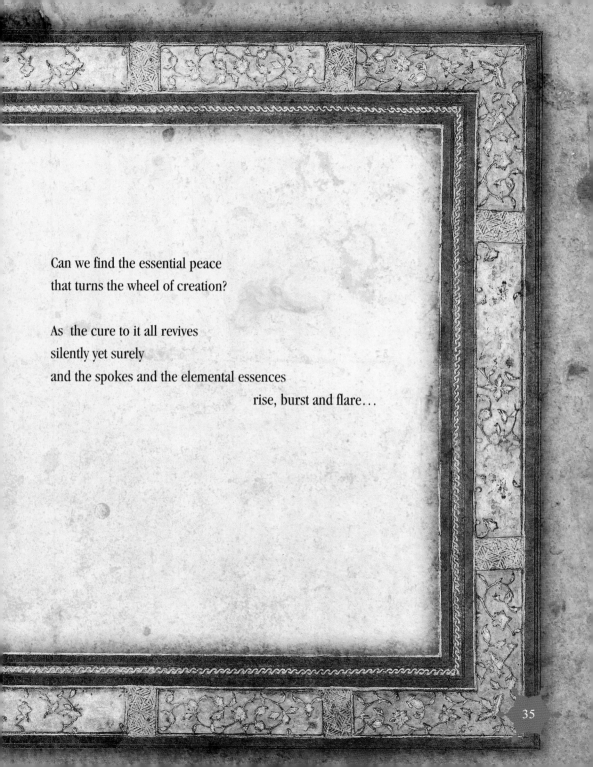

Can we find the essential peace
that turns the wheel of creation?

As the cure to it all revives
silently yet surely
and the spokes and the elemental essences

rise, burst and flare…

The Circle

In vain we circle
around the simple, the trivial
forgetting in the maze
that it is all a flicker in the candle of life

As flames surge
and the One, *as-Salam*
wipes it all
restoring the balance

His Names spoken softly
invoked passionately
sear our consciousness.

*as-Salam: The Peaceful One

Can You Hear Them

Can you listen with the inner ear
to their pleading whispers
their prayers
praising the One and Only

Can you hear
the leaves, roses, stones, woods
mountains, rivers, clouds and skies

His every living creature seeking His Love
shedding tears of need
till His Presence
overflows the tributaries of every pulsing vein
every living, pulsing cell
every source of temporal existence
with Elemental Serenity.

The Wheel

The wheel's turning
shadows love, lust, passions of this world
as it moves in a kaleidoscope of tumbling shards,

The illuminated soul
glistens within the circle of existence
as the music of the other realm
unheard and unseen by others
fills the soul with unbound joy

The empty threshold of this momentary station
is for once filled with golden lights
converging for once, converging
converging

The spokes of the wheel
lie at rest
the merging lights run off shaded shadows
and the circle is complete
                   is complete.

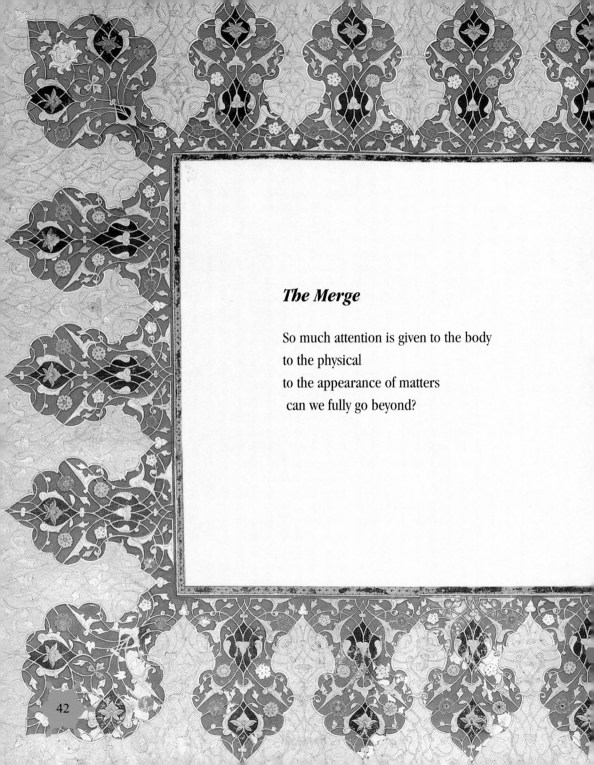

The Merge

So much attention is given to the body
to the physical
to the appearance of matters
 can we fully go beyond?

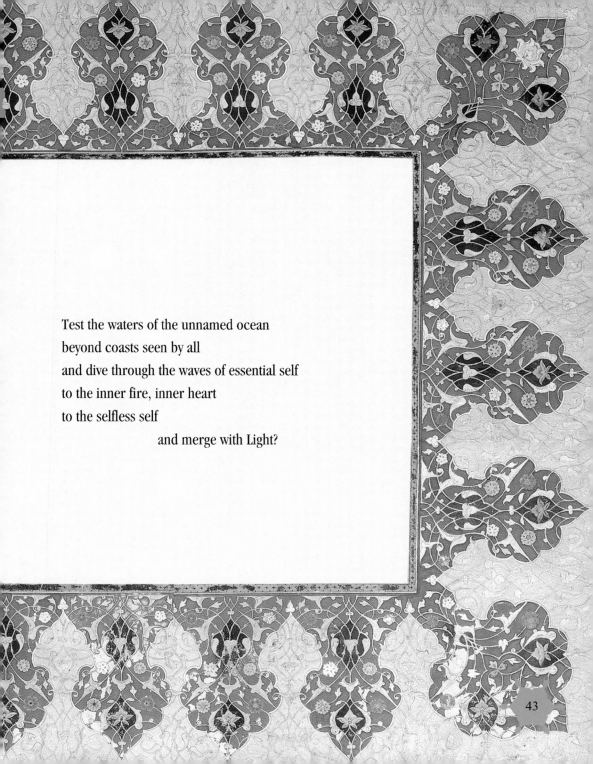

Test the waters of the unnamed ocean
beyond coasts seen by all
and dive through the waves of essential self
to the inner fire, inner heart
to the selfless self
                    and merge with Light?

CHAPTER TWO
THE INNER LAND

The Arena

Come,
come face to face
with yourself
rekindle the flame of truth

Look past the frayed, the marred
the stain of imposed dictated musts
let the chambers, walls and doors
implode into a new arena
where the face to face
brings forth a rebirth
and the Path Maker supersedes all.

Ripping The Veil

The aim of my search
What search?
is ever present on arising and falling asleep

As paths converge
and time descends with merciless claws
I sink deeper into questioning
deeper into visions
deeper into prayers
rejecting sleep, rejecting inhibitions
heartbeat raised, voice hushed,
tears a constant companion
till each hitched breath is a willing sacrifice
given freely, joyously

For my passing
without Your Love

without a glimpse of Your Beauty
without the feel of Your Grace
without the touch of Your Curing Presence
is not the search
it is the goal unbound, unveiled

The Unseen World is but an open doorway
to You, to You, to You
as the veil is finally torn aside

The shoreline of Hope is glimpsed
and time surrenders, melts away
as your Names of Power shine forth
taking on solidity and shape

A sparkling, potent web
of Eternal Love
embraces all,
                embraces all.

Divine Tapestry

The Message weaves its threads
intertwining tapestry of wisdom,
patched with light and mercy
As the sun sinks, I sink into Your Aura
Your Light, *noorak* enfolds, enrapts

Yaseen, at-Tawbah, Ar-Rahman
each a gem that never breaks
facets glisten with The Light
of the King of Kings

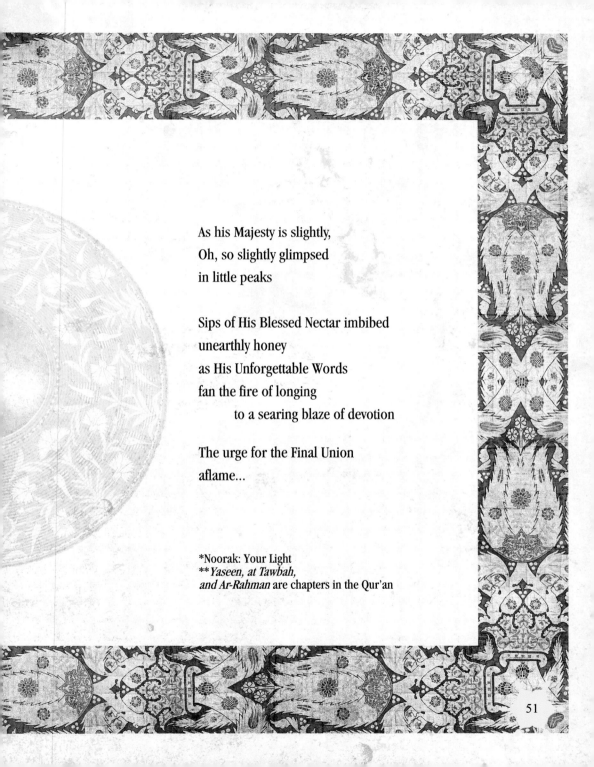

As his Majesty is slightly,
Oh, so slightly glimpsed
in little peaks

Sips of His Blessed Nectar imbibed
unearthly honey
as His Unforgettable Words
fan the fire of longing
       to a searing blaze of devotion

The urge for the Final Union
aflame...

*Noorak: Your Light
***Yaseen, at Tawbah,
and Ar-Rahman* are chapters in the Qur'an

The Power Within

Do we imprison ourselves purposely
with the temporal trends of existence?

Do we curry the favor of those who can turn aside
as the lustrous nets of passions pull them on ?

Do we deal death blows to hardened hearts
as they decay and solidify?

When the source of it all
can be felt simply by gazing deep
simply giving in
simply yielding
 to the power within.

What Stops the Joining?

Look deep, deeper within
the inner chambers of the soul
are the crevices of the core
as you join with the Beloved
in the inner core of your very being

With the power of prayer
awrad and *dua's*
welcoming doors welcome the soul
to its Ever-Evolving Temple.

The Inner Tablet

Do you see the writing on the inner tablet of the soul
where knowledge of the intangible resides
where the darkest darkness dissipates
where the cruelty of the friendless world dissolves
as we pass through the nine spheres
entering a nascent threshold
where realities turn and spin
with the turning of the stars
in the sought horizon of Ultimate Unity.

The Inner Homeland

In the homeland of the inner self
the breath quickens
held for a millisecond
in disbelief

Imprisoned
the despair in the breath let out
in a single instant

As faith pours
its healing humor
                        onto the parched soul.

His Will

When the rising current
turns into sorrowed struggles
chained, blocked passage
as man pulls out
torn, tattered lips pull back,
back arched, shaking, shuddering

His Will sets the currents flowing
rocks, corals leaves
falcons and eagles
revolve in circles of freedom
while human spirits seek the unknown
When the spirit of *ridha*, of acceptance ascends
the current flows

                in a soliloquy of mutual peace….

*Ridha: acceptance

Your Names

Alight on tongue and spirit
with their own shattering power

Revered names, qualities, powers
known and unknown
weave a core of power
that draws magnetically
bespells the lovers
in Irrefutable Unity
Peace sings out with serenity
in silent, ingrained, deepening tones

As your Powerful Names
encompass the present awakening
invoke future revelations
in a stream of potent
giving

As the core of existence
flares in sparks
raining bountifully in the Court of Rapture.

Drenched Dreams

Abandoning the false
scorning the empty husks of ego

I humble myself to your claim of my heart
Yearn for the reality
of dreams long drenched
in your Mercy.

Remnants and Rewards

The inner land of unrealities
teems with shades of truth and falsehood--

Tented, built, razed cities
abodes of pride through sequences of time
attest to those whose powers, thinking and ego
led them to believing their own construed truths
unmindful of the teachings
in the schools of oneness
unmindful of dignity
in the world of the downtrodden,
Yet the remnants of the remains
mutely mirror the insignificance of it all

Divine call throws off the mantles of darkness
and awakens the valleys of the trodden
with foretold rewards

Blissful benediction is sown across the valleys
and reaped forevermore
                      forevermore.

CHAPTER THREE
THE QUEST

Ultimate Quest

Looking down from on high
beyond the body
beyond this temporary shell
beyond the facades
beyond surroundings

The journey is one
of seeking the ultimate

Of peace, ease,
love of the Highest of the High
of the Supreme
crowning it all

With a surrender
a final unequivocal surrender
to Your Will.

Dream Encounters

Sleep eludes
the need for rest
set aside,
in Your Absence
tears wet my pillows
Your magnificence, shining visage
sets the yearning urge

Dreams of our Encounter
    in dreams
       fill my seeking soul

Will You watch from afar
    as the ache of missing steps up
      and visit one of these restless nights.

(Dedicated to Abiyyah Dabbagh, a dear friend and relative,inspired
by her wish to see our beloved Prophet, peace be upon him, in
dreams)

Race of Ultimates

As the nights of fasting ravel
threads and tapestries of prayers
of *thikr* combine

Days and nights speed on
as the net of time unravels
shedding the speedy hours
unheeding of the need to slow down

As teams of believers imbibe the blessings
an undeclared race carries them forth
pursuing the ultimate goals;
Unity, forgiveness, mercy
gifted medals of *thawab*,
conferred on the clamoring souls
in the Temple of the Hereafter
and the luster of the Nest of Heaven
shines   forth   in

        a welcoming, wondrous welcome.

* thawab: rewards
* thikr: devotional prayers of remembrance

Reaching the Light

Tonight the air thickens with loneliness
    Let's not bow down
Escape the ruins of a former glorious state
Run out of the open doorway of provoked thought
    Let's chant and dance
Listen to the internal music of the soul
    Unending chords of harmony
Dispel the spell of despair
As we reach out
On a quest for the Beloved's eternal
                      Light…

The Crescendo

The white pigeon croons in the early dawn hours
a song of praise, of *tasbeeh*
and hovering angels look down
serenading the All Powerful, All Merciful
as the figure on the cream carpet
sheds the weighty mantle of the world
eyes closed tight, lips rounding off preciously memorized dua's
heart rate raised in tandem with each heart-sent prayer

Prayers revolving
in a crescendo of need
spiral of seeking
breaking the loud silence silently
as the awaiting angles listen, join in and carry the message
welcoming, embracing the sight of the white-capped head
bowed head of the warrior
sitting so gracefully, elegantly
kneeling so serenely
bowed to the Beloved, unbowed to the world

Arms stretch wide as the white-covered shoulders
stay steady, firm, unyielding
and yet bowed only in reference to the Everlasting One
open palms raised
teary, tender eyes streaming with Supreme Love
in perfect utter Surrender to His Will.

*tasbeeh: invocations

77

It Is One Easy Stride

To losing oneself
as the traveler crosses the plains
and rides the steeds of passion
with vigor and fire

       It is an easy step
       a single breath
       a quiet action
       remember the courses
       crossings of youth and age
       remember the way stations
       as each leaves an imprint

Yet do not let the worries
drown out the carrying call
of the Ocean of Eternity
and dive, dive
dive....
till the tidal waves
        cradle you in everlasting peace.

The Seeker

He came out of the darkness
seeking light, enlightenment
seeking the path, the connection

Confident, a survivor of battles
unshakable, resolute
thousands of *awrad*, prayers
lift up his soul seeking Love for the One
dreams of *Al Habib* succor him
dwelling in the Beloved's presence
permeate his life, his journey

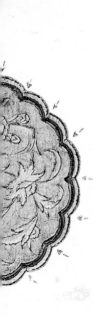

The Trustworthy pulls it all
and weaves with each prayer
a new beginning, a nascent path

Doors and mirrors reflect
his destiny

The homeland of peace calls out
as the wings of his soul
lift up and rise
to the dawn of a life of

                    Giving...

The Emergence

The rush of feet
beat of hearts
catch them in a maelstrom and tosses them
as seasons pass and scatter
into shadows colored with fading colors
of life, survival, trials and brilliant joys

Whispered songs carry them forth
their inner selves
hold secret yearnings
defeated and triumphant
in their own very beings
if and when they open up
and look past the rushing whirlwind
into the recesses of their severed selves
and embrace
contentment and gratitude
                            of countless blessings.

Your Gate

To sit down at Your doorstep
and call forth Your grace

To sit at Your gate of giving
and call forth Your protection
is but a service
that is still not fit to give You Your due

So when will it all fit,
and lead to the Union of souls?

Choices and Rewards

We seek Your signs
listen vigilantly for Your voice
pray for Your companionship
The Friend calls
as the whirling world
offers temporary power
to those whose ears are clogged
eyes shut to signs
seeking another passage
another journey
Yet the *Al Adil*, the Just
balances the power and giving
with Infinite Justice
unlike the blind justice of the unequal
as all is resolved
on The Day and along the path of *as-Sirat*
when all that matters is final unequivocal acceptance
and *Ridha* is beheld and celebrated
with consummate euphoria.

*as-Sirat:: the passage on the Day of Judgment
**Ridha: acceptance and forgiveness

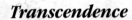

Transcendence

The world transcends
in a blink of eternity
from level to level, period to period
passages of recorded time
another flicker in eternity
we consider it all in proportion
or is it in proportion?

A second of existence
in the full scheme of half full lives
spent in devotion or devastation?

Cross the invisible bridge
between the realms
and look forward or back?

Cross the bridge
and enter with surety
the field beyond the mind's eye,
beyond faithless time lines
and resolve the Final Riddle of the Essence
as you step into the Homeland of Certainty.

CHAPTER FOUR
THE BRIDGE

The Waiting

The shallow shade of the body
is born in pain
awaiting
the Day of Return
when the robes of the cumbersome shell
are shed and shredded
to embrace
       the fullness of lighted, infinite joining.

The Hourglass

The balance sought
by each light seeker
the continual hunt
in the name of finding the lost elements
takes on facets through the eons
as eras speed by
years and centuries, but seconds and moments
in an invisible, powerful
unknown yet felt hourglass of the Beloved

The sands, pendulums, numbers
fade in and out
when the end approaches
The path carries the weight of each laden soul
in a flight only measured in timeless surrender
as the Eternal Honeymoon begins.

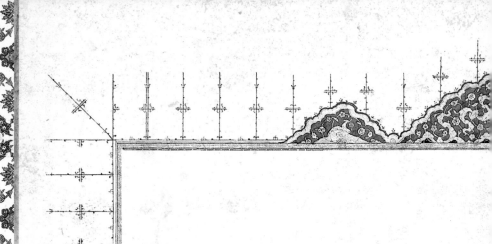

What Sets You Free

If the truth
doesn't set you free
If the truth doesn't expose you
don't enter the
River of Questing

Let the search take you elsewhere
delving, exploring the tributaries of life
And when you let it finally in
let it elevate you
and breathe in the musk of
Forgiveness, Acceptance
                    and rejoice!

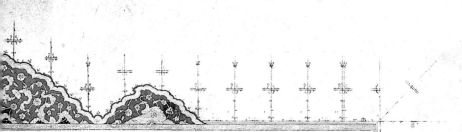

Seeds of Grace

Let's not shy away from the hidden
ignore the signs
wipe out dreams
each a seed of grace for those
with the mind's eye of gazing
into the very depth of eternal mystery
as they shake off the shackles of faceted facades
regaining the essence of all essences
and take up the torch of knowledge unbound.

Nightly Pilgrimage

We go on a pilgrimage
every night
with the turning of the sailing stars
and the dawn of the day
the pilgrimage of the soul
tugs and pulls
in the Realm of Love

Will the nightly pilgrimage
be observed?
will it be heeded?

Why even ask
it is more than enough
to make the ascension.

96

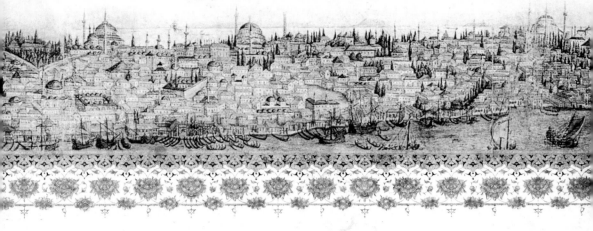

Nightly Devotions

The night after night journey
leaves the exhausted soul
seeking promised shelter
as rivers of desperation
as thankful palms are persistently raised
as chants, *salawat, takbirs* are raised
as His Names are passionately invoked

The turning of the planets
in the upper realm are but a minute happening
when the angels look down
and dive through the worlds to listen to souls
speeding on a flight of Devotional Rapture

*salawat: prayers
**takbirs: proclaiming the greatness of the One

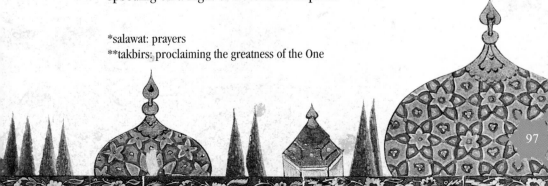

97

Language of the Spirit

Do we sink into the rapture
of the pursuit
and take up the persistent call
of the inner being
as the language of the spirit
written in invisible script
silently cries out to be heeded
as the residence of the inner core
beckons gently
and stamps its imprint.

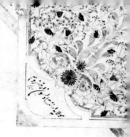

Finding the Source

To find the one not found
in a world of intransients
is it a possible task
to find the completion
in this brief instance?

To balance with the heart's sense
the unrelenting, yearning for The Source
in an abode where opposites merge
created just for us
just for us,
Is it ever possible
to give enough thanks
moving through *Dar al-Qurur*, the World of Pride
unfettered, unburdened
by the encroaching darkness of cumbersome burdens
and passing through the gracious gates
                    of *Dar as-Salam*

Permanence

What is permanence in an impermanent world?
can the cloud of certainty remain full
with the promise of permanence
catching each weeping, sky bound prayer?

Can the rainfall of promising benediction
enrich the soil of seeking souls
plant and root the light of benevolence?

Will the compassion of His Munificence
stroke each helpless, questing soul
in promised Eternal Love

When his Fire of Mercy
rains like waterfalls of descending deliverance
and the clouds dissipate to reveal
the Enduring Sun of all Suns.

Soul Sailors

The emptiness seeps in
as the ocean of the forsaken
sends a siren's call out

Caught in a silken net of soulful hunger
sailors drenched in questing desire
yearn in utter soul wrenching need for your favor
As the sails of countless gossamer floating abodes
ring with the cries of agreeable slaves
welcoming and ardently bowing
in blissful ecstasy
to the Captain of all Worlds
steering countless souls
through the heavenly still
      Ocean
       of the Ever After.

CHAPTER FIVE

THE JOURNEY

The Journey of All Journeys

The journey is tedious
the journey is worrisome
the journey is prohibitive
the journey is beyond the expected
as we each step onto planned and unplanned quests
we forget the decisive journey
the journey into the self
and face the mirror
of His Crowning Glory

Take the journey
and greet His Unceasing Love
fold away all false mirrors and masks
as you fervently claim the inner pilgrimage.

The Realm of Seekers

Will the darkness of despair
seeping across the canvas of the soul
glow with benediction?

Will the thunderous needs
of the weak and wearied
be nullified with strength?

Will the battle-weary warriors of light
heal their wounds
carry the torch of forgiven and benedicted spirits
and surge onwards, onwards, onwards
in the glimmering realm of the Seekers?

Living Landscape of Souls

The living landscape of our souls
extends a welcome
as every curved letter, word, verse, chapter
sends forth peace,
Light upon light
nooron 'ala noor
The Beloved's light
glints through the pages of time

A friend leading us to The Friend
we imbibe Your Flavor through our thirsty souls
gain messages of mercy, wisdom, succor, ease
through the Storybook of all
The melodies of Your Voice guide us
an aim for the aimless
guiding galaxy stars turn away in shame
a million suns dim
in acquiescent respect of Your Light
Light upon light
nooron 'ala noor

Soaring, uplifting recitations resound
as the very foundations of our inner center
fall silent in humble obedience
with *al kalimat al tammat,* "the Whole Words"
and embrace
the Sacred text in utter Submission
Your Majesty of Light
brushes the landscape of our soul
we traverse this existence through
the guiding light
nooron 'ala noor
Light upon light
nooron 'ala noor

Sought Stations

Moving onwards to stations sought
invisible yet solid
        to the spirit's eye

Sifting through layers,
layers upon layers
levels beyond known and unknown domains
        reaching the Nest of Heaven

As we seek dreams of meeting *Al Habib*
within the mists of the unrealized realm
and his revered cloak weaves
in and out of reality

Visions carry our woven souls
onto the flawless tapestry of unified souls
presented to the Supreme Beloved.

Al Habib: Prophet Muhammad peace be upon him

The Wise One

Can they rise past the defeat
of severed selves
to discover the secrets long held
in eyes shining with inner noor
of wise souls
living, imbibing, embracing the light
of acceptance
of self-separation
on their unassuming journeys
of love for the Beloved
holding onto the sheerest of silken webs
to this strange existence
while awaiting the time
of Ultimate Unity
with patience and inner smiles
welcoming hidden knowledge
a bond beyond all
as they tread the path of seekers?

Dedicated to brother Shems Friedlander

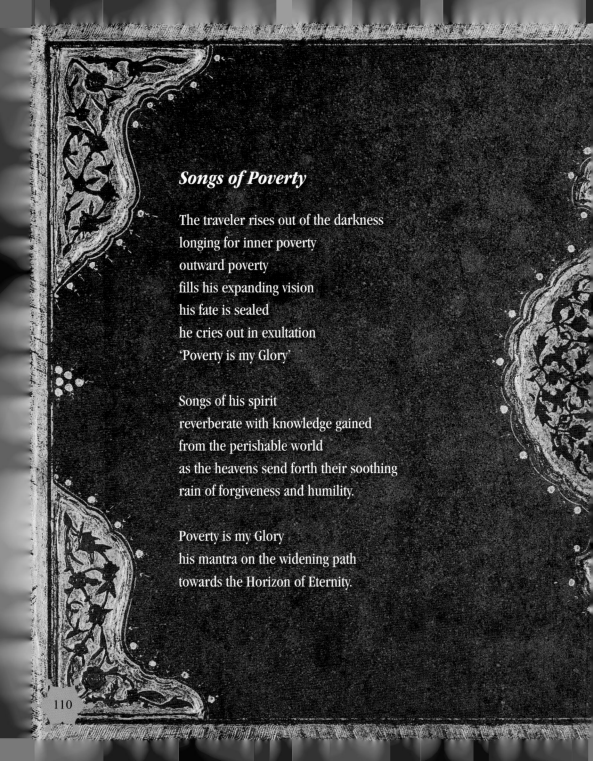

Songs of Poverty

The traveler rises out of the darkness
longing for inner poverty
outward poverty
fills his expanding vision
his fate is sealed
he cries out in exultation
'Poverty is my Glory'

Songs of his spirit
reverberate with knowledge gained
from the perishable world
as the heavens send forth their soothing
rain of forgiveness and humility.

Poverty is my Glory
his mantra on the widening path
towards the Horizon of Eternity.

Sips on the Journey

Hand stitched with prayers, with reverence
verses embroidered in golden glory

Golden threads stand out in stark relief
framed on woven black,
subliminal black embroidery with every hand span
black and gold, gold and black

His House
solid,
square,
circled by feet, hand, hearts, souls
passing the seven heavens
millions upon millions
timeless splendor, timeless surrender

Crying, weeping visages
look up and down
as they seek the Union
casting away stiff shackles of fluctuating life
a rebirth and a death
A heady mindboggling mix
of serenity, peace
                    descends.

Conquering Grace

They seek to hijack
our love for Your Mercy
connection to Your Light
with stern sermons
raging voices
harsh visages
to rip the serenity
of uplifting meditation
awaiting a surrender
that never comes
as the banner of boundless grace
ripples by dawn and into the night
and love beyond perception
conquers all
triumphantly dancing a victorious victory.

Dawn Messages, Dawn Prayers

As the sleepless soul
steps into the heavenly garden
under the healing rays of the everlasting Sun
the flute strings bow in flagrant joy
every lilt in honor
of dawn-filled nights
of pure prayers sent on the wings of late nights
with the first white threads of dawn
delivering them to the Lord of the Worlds
in humble, wondrous giving.

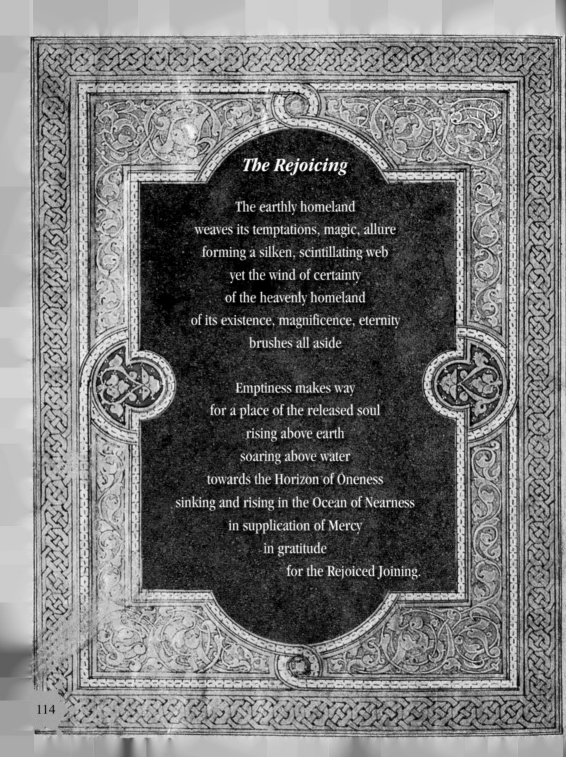

The Rejoicing

The earthly homeland
weaves its temptations, magic, allure
forming a silken, scintillating web
yet the wind of certainty
of the heavenly homeland
of its existence, magnificence, eternity
brushes all aside

Emptiness makes way
for a place of the released soul
rising above earth
soaring above water
towards the Horizon of Oneness
sinking and rising in the Ocean of Nearness
in supplication of Mercy
in gratitude
for the Rejoiced Joining.

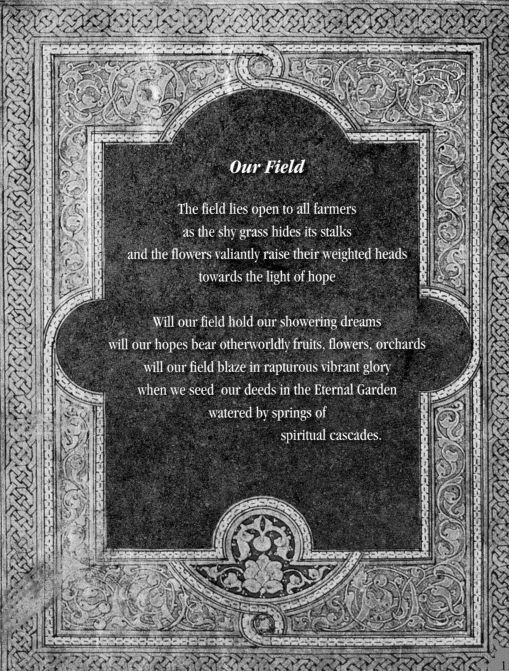

Our Field

The field lies open to all farmers
as the shy grass hides its stalks
and the flowers valiantly raise their weighted heads
towards the light of hope

Will our field hold our showering dreams
will our hopes bear otherworldly fruits, flowers, orchards
will our field blaze in rapturous vibrant glory
when we seed our deeds in the Eternal Garden
watered by springs of
spiritual cascades.

Shaking Off the Dust

The mold constrains
of mud,
from mud
to dust

Scattered souls
scattered bits
flimsy wisps

That is the reality
from earth to earth, dust to dust
can we remember
that it is all, all, all
a millisecond of existence
as we pray for the final meeting
beseech your Mighty Mercy
to enter the Everlasting Haven

From dust to dust
we fly on and descend
on short, cropped wings
the cage, a temporary holding cell
and

      shake off the
        dust……

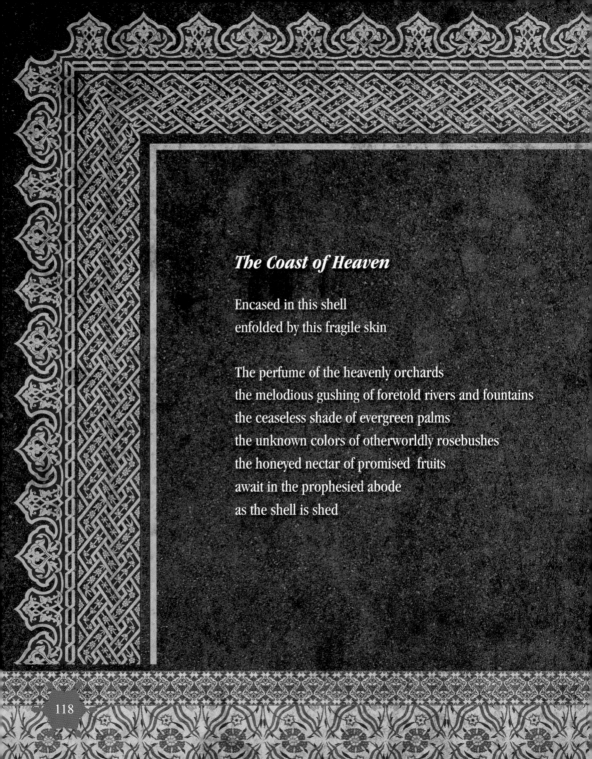

The Coast of Heaven

Encased in this shell
enfolded by this fragile skin

The perfume of the heavenly orchards
the melodious gushing of foretold rivers and fountains
the ceaseless shade of evergreen palms
the unknown colors of otherworldly rosebushes
the honeyed nectar of promised fruits
await in the prophesied abode
as the shell is shed

Heading straight to the heart of yearned destinations
the pearly homes, beloved visages of Prophets
where angels and heavenly creatures
blessedly reside
landing and settling on
                    the Coast of Heaven.

PICTURE CREDITS